SOUTHE┋ TROLLEYBUSES

Colin Barker

Series editor Robert J Harley

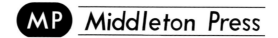
MP Middleton Press

This publication is dedicated to the late Clarence Carter, whose photographs have given so much pleasure to untold transport enthusiasts over the years, not only in his choice of subject, but also in location and quality of reproduction. His work, which enhanced so many publications, will be greatly missed.

Published August 2012
First Reprinted January 2013

ISBN 978 1 908174 20 8

© Middleton Press, 2012

Design Deborah Esher

Published by
  Middleton Press
  Easebourne Lane
  Midhurst
  West Sussex
  GU29 9AZ
Tel: 01730 813169
Fax: 01730 812601
Email: info@middletonpress.co.uk
www.middletonpress.co.uk

Printed in the United Kingdom by Henry Ling Limited, at the Dorset Press, Dorchester, DT1 1HD

CONTENTS

INTRODUCTION AND ACKNOWLEDGMENTS

Southend was one of the early municipalities to introduce trolleybuses, and vehicles purchased over the years proved to be interesting. Early double deck deliveries had the driver's cab protruding from the main body, to be followed by those with a full front and dummy motorbus style radiator. Other pre-war deliveries included the sole trolleybus manufactured by the Gloucester Railway Carriage and Wagon Company, and a front entrance AEC "Q" type that was one of only five produced.

During the war some vehicles were loaned to Bradford, which led to this municipality adopting a blue and cream livery, said to be inspired by Southend's colours. To cope with postwar summer traffic second hand trolleybuses were purchased, and two of the fleet were converted into mobile vehicles after withdrawal. One was a mobile radar unit for the fledgling Southend Airport, and the other a public convenience.

This publication is not intended to be a detailed history of the system, but more a pictorial journey along the routes the trolleybuses served. One of the biggest problems for the undertaking was the imbalance of traffic between winter, and the great influx of summer holidaymakers and day-trippers.

Thanks go to the photographers, copyright holders and individual collection owners for the generous use of their material, and due accreditation has been given with each view where known. I have been unable to trace the origin of some views; I hope the photographers accept their work has added to the visual presentation of this album. Unfortunately I never saw the system in operation, but local enthusiasts Dennis Gill (who rode to and from school on the trolleybuses), Peter Clark and Richard Delahoy (author of *Southend Corporation Transport* published in 1986) have been of great assistance by kindly agreeing to read through the first draft manuscript; their input has been invaluable. The line drawings are by Terry Russell, map prepared by Roger Smith, ticket supplied by Eric Old, and the timetables/fare charts via staff at the Omnibus Society Library, Walsall. My thanks to them for their assistance.

Finally, yet again, thanks must go to my wife Maureen, who helped with my research visits to Southend, and who used her computer skills to convert my handiwork into a usable format for the publisher.

HISTORICAL AND
GEOGRAPHICAL SETTING

Southend-on-Sea is situated on the north shore of the Thames Estuary, with the low lying lands towards Shoeburyness/Foulness Island to the east, and northwards towards the River Roach. Local cliffs lead to higher ground to the west in the direction of Leigh-on-Sea and Hadleigh.

In the 15th century, Prittlewell, located slightly to the north, was the centre of activity and the local manor owned the land down to the edge of the estuary, the area being known as the South End of the estate. In the 18th century, this area became one where people could bathe in the waters for health reasons. From this small beginning, and the earlier activities of oyster fishermen, the town developed with property initially hugging the shoreline.

Promoters vied with Brighton to attract visitors from London, but transport was difficult unless you owned your own carriage. The river offered no help with its extensive mud flats, and in 1828 landowners formed The Southend Pier Company to provide a landing stage for small vessels. Royal Assent was given in March 1829, and work commenced almost immediately. The pier was of wooden construction and extended in stages for 1.25 miles (2.01 km), incorporating a horse drawn tramway. The promoters could not keep up with the mortgage repayments and the structure was sold by public auction to a local syndicate who were interested in developing the pier head area.

The London, Tilbury and Southend Railway (LTS) arrived in the town in 1856 and this, plus the river traffic, greatly increased summer trippers, especially from London's East End. The land between the LTS (now Central) Station and the estuary was ripe for development, and in 1866 the Southend Local Board was formed to take over responsibility for many aspects of local government.

By 1876, Southend had grown to include the areas of Prittlewell, Chalkwell and Westcliff, becoming a borough in September 1892, and changing its name to Southend-on-Sea in 1893; County Borough status was granted in 1914.

The arrival of the Great Eastern Railway (GER) in 1889 provided a second station (now Victoria), which resulted in an even greater influx of summer visitors.

The wooden pier structure had declined over the years leading to the abandonment of the horse tramway. An Act of Parliament authorised a steel replacement, which was partially opened in 1889. A third rail electric tramway was provided over the lengthened pier, the latter giving access to larger vessels, thus further adding to the visitor traffic.

By 1897, when Southchurch was incorporated into the borough, the population had grown to around 23,000 and was rapidly increasing. This growth led to the consideration of some form of public transport, and the electrification of the pier tramway was probably the catalyst.

HISTORICAL BACKGROUND
TO PUBLIC TRANSPORT

Powers were sought by Southend Council under the Light Railways Act of 1896 to open a tramway system in the borough, and following a public inquiry three routes were sanctioned. These were from Leigh to Southchurch via Victoria Circus, from Southchurch Road to Marine Parade, and from High Street to London Road via Prittlewell.

Work started in 1900 incorporating single track and passing loops to a 3ft 6in (1067mm) gauge. The low railway bridge in the High Street meant that cars could only operate to the north of the obstruction, and this problem would remain during the trolleybus era. Progress was slow and the system was eventually opened on 19th July 1901 with twelve double deck and two single deck cars.

Traffic exceeded expectations, especially in the summer months, and further cars were purchased between 1902 and 1924, plus seven second hand vehicles in 1934. Track was extended in a number of stages to Thorpe Bay, the final stage being completed in February 1912. Construction of Thorpe Bay and Southchurch Boulevards provided off road central reservation running, and the creation of circular routes from the town centre by July 1914.

To improve frequency, double track was installed between 1907 and 1920, but not before the North Road section of the London Road via Prittlewell route had been cut back in stages to the Blue Boar by June 1921. Finally, tracks were provided for the Corporation's landing pier and around Warrior Square, the latter becoming an important town centre terminus. For a more detailed survey of the Southend tramway system, the Middleton Press *Southend-on-Sea Tramways* by Robert J Harley is recommended.

The Prittlewell route did not figure in the track dualling programme, and thoughts turned to other means of improving frequencies, namely the use of trolleybuses, although at that time Southend did not have the necessary powers. The Ministry of Transport allowed a one year experiment, so two Railless single deckers were hired, running from Victoria Circus along Victoria Avenue to the Blue Boar, and thus supplementing the existing tram frequency. The first of the hired vehicles entered service on 16th October 1925, and the route was extended the following year to Priory Park ready for the Whitsun holiday traffic.

Trolleybus powers were incorporated in the Corporation Act of 1926, and a third AEC single decker hired in 1927. The low seating capacity of the first three hired vehicles, which were subsequently purchased, was a problem, so a double deck Garrett was hired in January 1928; this was also purchased. It proved to be a success and a further five were ordered, the Prittlewell trams being withdrawn in December 1928. It had been hoped that trolleybuses could travel along the north section of High Street from Victoria Circus and terminate in the forecourt of the LTS (by now LMS) Station. This was refused by the railway company, so wiring was erected from High Street along Whitegate Road to a reverser with the junction of Bankside. Wiring was subsequently erected along the latter, Seaway and Marine Parade to terminate at the Kursaal.

Two three-axle English Electric (EEC) trolleybuses were purchased in 1930, followed in 1932/33 by a further nine two-axle models by AEC/EEC, plus a three-axle ex-demonstrator from the same source. Although trolleybuses were being introduced, a tram refurbishment programme was running in parallel.

In January 1932, an extension from Priory Park along Fairfax Drive and Cavendish Gardens to Eastwood Boulevard was opened, and in July of the same year a route from Victoria Circus to Hamstel Road via North Avenue commenced; trams had not operated along either of these inland roads, but they continued on remaining routes. A short extension along Marine Parade to the pier head was opened in the summer of 1934. In the same year the two rare vehicles mentioned in the introduction were also acquired.

In July 1935, wiring was extended along Nelson Road from Eastwood Boulevard to its junction with Wellington Avenue where a reverser was installed; this was only a short distance from the London Road tram route to Leigh.

It was now apparent that trolleybuses would replace the remaining trams, and the route from Kursaal to Thorpe Bay, which was originally intended to reach Shoeburyness, was converted from 27th May 1939; it was soon withdrawn with the advent of the Second World War. This also prevented the delivery of a reported order for 30 plus AECs to cover fleet replacement and route extensions; the order was not pursued after the end of hostilities. However, in the same year six AEC two-axle vehicles were added to the fleet, four of which were loaned to Bradford City Transport between September 1942 and February 1943. April 1942 saw the closure of the tramway system, with London Road converted to trolleybuses as far as its junction with Nelson Road, providing western circular routes from Victoria Circus. Secondly, the conversion of the routes along Southchurch Avenue to the Kursaal, and along Southchurch Road to the White Horse public house completed the picture by 1944.

In June 1943, a single loop around Warrior Square came into use, plus a single line connection along Milton Street from its junction with Bradley Street, to gain access to the square. The final extension was along Hamstel Road in April 1944, providing a connection between Southchurch Road and North Avenue, allowing the creation of the eastern circular routes, resulting in a maximum route mileage of 11.2 miles (18.0 km).

The years 1945/46 saw the delivery of nine utility Sunbeams, which were eventually sold to Doncaster Corporation. Also acquired were five Leyland single deckers ex-Tees-side Railless Traction Board to help with increased summer traffic immediately after the end of the war, creating a maximum fleet strength of 32. The fleet was further supplemented with the purchase of nine Sunbeams from Wolverhampton Corporation in 1950, which allowed some older vehicles to be withdrawn.

A number of factors led to the decline and eventual closure of the trolleybus system. The nationalisation of the electricity supply industry in 1948 resulting in increased costs, the development of postwar housing estates, the greater flexibility of motorbuses and the increasing cost of overhead equipment all contributed. However, another major factor was the creation of a comprehensive working agreement between the Corporation, Westcliff-on-Sea Motor Services and Eastern National, which after some earlier setbacks, was implemented on 2nd January 1955.

By the early 1950s the Kursaal services had ceased. The East Circulars closed on 10th February 1954 and final system closure came on 28th October 1954, when the West Circulars were replaced by motorbuses. This ended 53 years of electric powered street public transport in the town, with trolleybuses contributing 29 years.

SERVICE NUMBERS
(USED FROM AROUND 1949)

28	Town Centre - Chalkwell Schools (Wellington Avenue). 28 not always shown
28A	West Circular outward via London Road (clockwise)
28B	West Circular outward via Victoria Avenue (anti-clockwise)
28C	Priory Park - Kursaal (workman service)
51	Town Centre - Kursaal via Southchurch Avenue
51A	Town Centre - Thorpe Bay via Southchurch Avenue/Kursaal (summer only)
52	Town Centre - Kursaal via Seaway/Marine Parade
52A	Town Centre - Thorpe Bay via Seaway/Kursaal (summer only)
63	Warrior Square - Southchurch
63A	East Circular outward via North Avenue (clockwise)
63B	East Circular outward via Southchurch Road (anti-clockwise)

Liveries

Original	Green and Cream/Ivory with lining out in various styles
Final	Light Blue and Cream

Abbreviations

AEC	Associated Equipment Company (manufacturers of bus and trolleybus chassis)
BTH	British Thomson-Houston (manufacturers of trolleybus electrical equipment)
EEC	English Electric Company (manufacturers of trolleybuses, electrical equipment & bodywork)
GEC	General Electric Company (manufacturers of trolleybus electrical equipment)
GER	Great Eastern Railway
LMS	London Midland and Scottish Railway
LNER	London and North Eastern Railway
LTPS	London Trolleybus Preservation Society
LTS	London, Tilbury and Southend Railway
NTA	National Trolleybus Association
OTA	Online Transport Archive
TLRS	Tramway and Light Railway Society
UK	United Kingdom

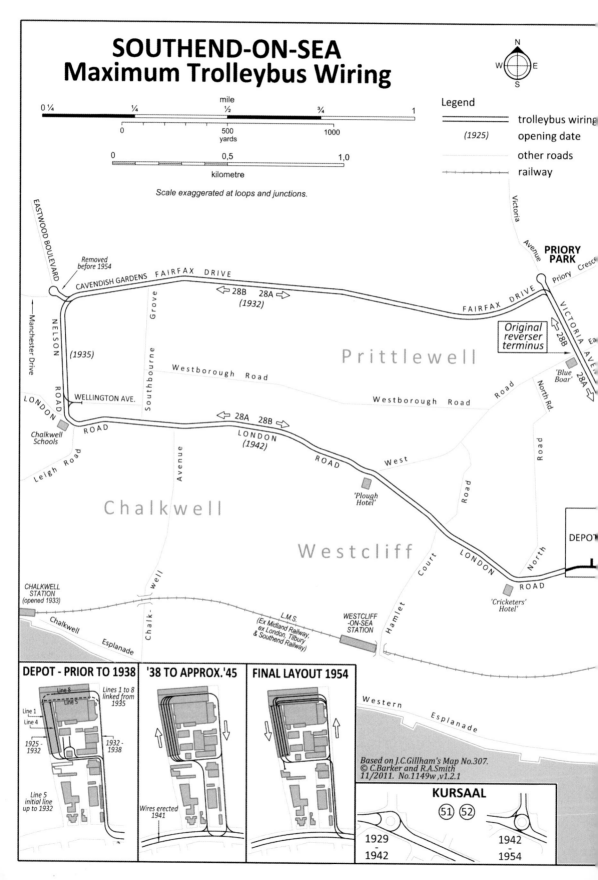

SOUTHEND-ON-SEA
Maximum Trolleybus Wiring

Legend

════════	trolleybus wiring
(1925)	opening date
———	other roads
+++++	railway

mile
0 ¼   ¼   ½   ¾   1

0   500   1000
yards

0   0,5   1,0
kilometre

Scale exaggerated at loops and junctions.

EASTWOOD BOULEVARD

Removed before 1954

CAVENDISH GARDENS   FAIRFAX DRIVE

⇐ 28B   28A ⇒
(1932)

Priory Cresc
PRIORY PARK

Victoria Avenue

FAIRFAX DRIVE

VICTORIA AVE

Ea

28B

Original reverser terminus

Manchester Drive

NELSON ROAD

(1935)

Grove

Southbourne

Westborough   Road

P r i t t l e w e l l

Road

North Rd.

28A ⇒

'Blue Boar'

WELLINGTON AVE.

LONDON   ROAD

Westborough   Road

Road

Chalkwell Schools

Leigh Road

Avenue

⇐ 28A   28B ⇒

LONDON
(1942)

ROAD

West

Road

C h a l k w e l l

'Plough Hotel'

W e s t c l i f f

LONDON ROAD

North

DEPOT

well

Court

Hamlet

'Cricketers' Hotel'

ROAD

CHALKWELL STATION
(opened 1933)

Chalk-

Chalkwell   Esplanade

L.M.S.
(Ex Midland Railway,
ex London, Tilbury
& Southend Railway)

WESTCLIFF-ON-SEA STATION

DEPOT - PRIOR TO 1938

Line 8
Lines 1 to 8 linked from 1935
Line 5
Line 1
Line 4
1925 - 1932
1932 - 1938
Line 5 initial line up to 1932

'38 TO APPROX.'45

Wires erected 1941

FINAL LAYOUT 1954

Western   Esplanade

*Based on J.C.Gillham's Map No.307.
© C.Barker and R.A.Smith
11/2011. No.1149w ,v1.2.1*

KURSAAL

51 52

1929 - 1942

1942 - 1954

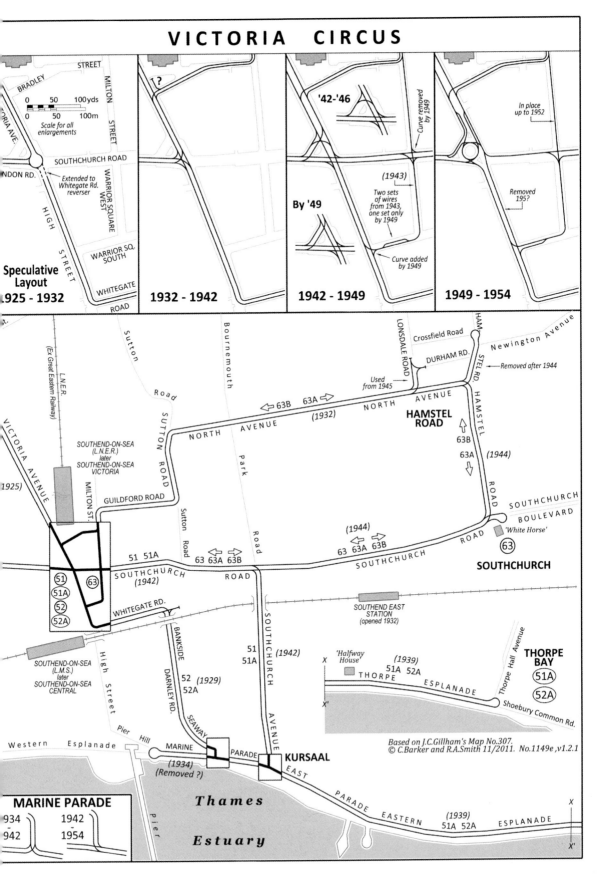

TRAM AND TROLLEYBUS ERA

Southend ran both trams and trolleybuses for a period of 16½ years from 1925 until 1942, rather than the latter being a rapid replacement for the track based vehicles, as was the case in many other municipalities. In fact, when trolleybuses were first introduced a tram refurbishment programme was in progress.

1.   In this view, trams 21 and 67 pass each other at Victoria Circus on their respective journeys to Southchurch and Leigh-on-Sea, with the Garon store on the left, and the Victoria Hotel on the right. There is a mixture of tram and trolleybus overhead wiring, with the latter running from High Street on the right to Victoria Avenue on the left, and onwards to Prittlewell/Priory Park. Trolleybus wiring also runs from the facing Southchurch Road into Victoria Avenue and from High Street into London Road, which is to the rear of the photographer. The former was probably an interim arrangement pending the final layout. (Commercial Postcard/Author's collection)

2.   Tram and trolleybus wiring is again illustrated in this view in Eastern Esplanade, just east of the Kursaal, and probably taken in the third quarter of 1939. This section of road was earlier known as East Parade. The boom of Car 66 is just about to be put to the overhead, which is pulled off to the traction standard to the rear, adjacent to the Army and Navy public house. The trolleybus overhead continues on towards Thorpe Bay. The menu of the restaurant next to the fish and chip establishment includes egg and chips at 6d (2.5p) and salmon and cucumber for 8d (3.5p). (W J Haynes)

3.   This view, from the mid 1930s includes three forms of passenger transport passing through Victoria Circus. Car 25 is about to leave London Road, with one of the Garrett six wheel trolleybuses passing in front and about to enter High Street on a return trip from Priory Park. In the period until the trams finished, the overhead linesmen had a difficult task in maintaining the mixed overhead. A Westcliff-on-Sea motorbus completes the picture. (Author's collection)

VICTORIA CIRCUS

4.   Victoria Circus was the hub of the Southend trolleybus system, with the majority of the services passing through, and with the final 1949 wiring around the traffic island allowing approaching vehicles to travel in any one of four directions. This view is looking north along Victoria Avenue, with an ex Wolverhampton Sunbeam trolleybus passing the Municipal College

as it leaves London Road to join two other vehicles on stand. In the distance is the former Public Library, now a museum, with Victoria Railway Station to the right, and showing evidence of steam motive power. A trolleybus leaves Bradley Street from the eastern part of the town. All the buildings in the foreground, and the entrance to Victoria Avenue, have been swept away to be replaced by the Odeon cinema, the Victoria Plaza Shopping Centre and Queensway Ring Road. (D Gill)

5.   This view depicts AEC 127 in a similar position to that in the previous picture, although it is travelling under wiring leading around the traffic island. From here, 127 can travel forward into Southchurch Road, return along London Road from which it has emerged or, for a short period after 1949, turn into High Street. An entrance to Victoria Arcade can be seen on the right, and the Corona brand has stood the test of time. (D Gill)

➜   6. The conductor of Sunbeam 150 (ex-Wolverhampton 271) enjoys a quick breather before reaching the next stop. The gantry on which the booms are mounted can be clearly seen, with cabling in front running down to the driver's cab.   150 also carries a Corona advertisement, and is closely followed by a Southend utility Daimler motorbus on service 61B. This area is now pedestrianised.
(D Gill)

➜   7. Sunbeam 147 (ex Wolverhampton 267) enters Victoria Circus from the northerly Victoria Avenue on Service 63B, the anti-clockwise East Circular. It is under the nearside wiring and will shortly turn left into Southchurch Road, then on to the White Horse and Hamstel Road. The offside overhead leads onto the 360 degree wiring around the traffic island.
(W J Haynes/NTA collection)

8.	The EEC winged motif, with AEC badge below, stands out on the dummy radiator of 115 as it moves down the eastern side of the Circus past Garons store. The destination shows Hamstel Road via High Street, but 115 is travelling in the opposite direction; perhaps the blind has been changed in anticipation of the return journey. Note the style of child's pushchair, and that traffic now warrants a policeman on point duty. (Omnibus Society collection)

➔	9. Sunbeam 146 (ex-Wolverhampton 266) has left Victoria Avenue, and travels around the southern side of the Circus before entering London Road, on the clockwise circuit of the West Circular. The substantial Garons store provides the backdrop, advertising groceries and confectionery, together with a teashop. A Ford Popular, and a Southend Massey bodied AEC motorbus, complete the picture. (D Thompson)

➔	10. The trolleybuses purchased ex-Tees-side Railless Traction Board in 1946 increased the fleet to cope with the immediate post war influx of holidaymakers and day trippers; here we see Leyland 139 (ex Tees-side 9). The vehicle rounds the southern side of the traffic island in this 1950 picture, with the Garons store on the right. These single deckers were mainly used on the services from the town centre to the Kursaal, but could, on occasions, be found on other areas of the system. (C Carter/LTPS)

11. AEC 128 rounds the western side of the traffic island before reaching the Victoria Avenue stand of Service 28B, the anti-clockwise West Circular. The corner of Garons store can be seen on the immediate left, with Southchurch Road beyond and the Victoria Hotel opposite. To the rear is Dixon's imposing store, now occupied by W H Smith. The addition of flowerbeds has reduced the starkness of the traffic island, while 128 travels under modern rigid twin line hangers. (W J Haynes)

→ 12. Utility Sunbeam W 138 leaves High Street and passes across Victoria Circus before entering Victoria Avenue on its way to Priory Park. Thus the Southchurch Road/London Road wiring was crossed at 90 degrees before the traffic island referred to earlier was installed. This vehicle, like the rest of the batch, was sold to Doncaster Corporation in 1954, becoming 392 in their fleet. After operating them in original condition, Doncaster overhauled the chassis and had the batch rebodied by Roe. Following eventual withdrawal in 1961/62, the bodies were converted to half cab configuration and fitted to Daimler motorbus chassis.
(W J Haynes/NTA collection)

→ 13. At the same location in the early years of the system, Garrett 105 is about to cross the entrance to Southchurch Road, and then pass the Victoria Hotel to enter High Street. Note the public conveniences in the centre of the Circus, the absence of the Garon store clock tower, and the early livery style with much greater areas of cream/ivory. (D S Giles/Omnibus Society copyright)

14.　　This late afternoon shot of AEC-EEC 112 depicts the rebuilt format, minus the original dummy radiator, but still retaining the piano front and twin destination indicators.　It is parked on the western side of the triangle that existed before the traffic island was created, and under wiring that led into London Road.
(W J Haynes/NTA collection)

➜　15. On a warm summer's day in 1949, AEC 129 is seen outside the Municipal College with the destination showing Chalkwell Schools, but with the slip board clarifying it is a circular. At this time (1946-1951), the western end of the system ran as circulars via Victoria Circus; prior to this vehicles looped round Warrior Square and High Street. A separate service was also running between Warrior Square and Priory Park.　To the rear is AEC motorbus 243 (ex-Mansfield District Traction 58) destined for Leigh-on-Sea; it will circumnavigate the traffic island, and pick up on the south side of London Road.
(C Carter/LTPS)

➜　16. This view depicts AEC 124 on stand at the beginning of London Road with Victoria Circus in the immediate background.　The Garon store, complete with clock tower, lies beyond and the Municipal College is to the left.　The vehicle is on Service 28A, the clockwise circuit of the West Circular.　(R F Mack/NTA collection)

WEST CIRCULAR

The West Circular developed in the following four stages.

Stage 1   *Opening service from town centre to Prittlewell from
16th October 1925, with an extension to Priory Park the following
Whitsun. First section of eventual tram replacement.*

Stage 2   *From Priory Park along Fairfax Drive and Cavendish Gardens to
Eastwood Boulevard from 21st January 1932.*

Stage 3   *From Eastwood Boulevard along Nelson Road to Wellington Avenue
from 24th July 1935.*

Stage 4   *From Wellington Avenue junction along the remainder of Nelson Road,
and then via London Road to Victoria Circus following closure of the
tramway system on 8th April 1942.*

The next picture sequence follows these stages.

Victoria Avenue/Prittlewell/Priory Park

17.   The imposing façade of the Boys High School (later the Municipal College), which was
demolished in 1971, forms the backdrop for this view of one of the original Railless single deck
trolleybuses that opened the system on 16th October 1925. Two were initially hired from the
manufacturer to run north in parallel with the trams along Victoria Avenue to Prittlewell Blue
Boar, increasing the frequency over the route, which had single tram track with passing loops.
The trams started from High Street, but the trolleybuses turned short at Victoria Circus to avoid
overcomplicating the overhead wiring, and because of the difficulty in turning in the former
thoroughfare. The route was later extended to the gates of Priory Park in 1926, and south to Marine
Parade and the Kursaal in 1929. The driver had no weather protection, and the solid tyres would
have given passengers a hard ride. (J B Atkinson/A B Cross collection)

18.   AEC-EEC 113 has lost its dummy radiator and piano front to be replaced with the smooth lines indicated. It is depicted on stand at the beginning of Victoria Avenue in 1954, with Victoria Circus off to the left, and is under the nearside wiring, having arrived from London Road. The eastern side of the Municipal College looks very imposing, but the rear elevation less so. (C Carter/LTPS)

TROLLEYBUS FARE TABLE.
Eastwood Boulevard Route.

STAGE							
1	Kursaal						
2	1d	(Whitegate Road) Bankside					
3	1d	1d	Southend L.M.S.R. and L.N.E.R. Stations				
4	2d	2d	1d	Priory Park			
5	2d	2d	1½d	1d	Shakespeare Drive		
6	2½d	2½d	2d	1d	1d	Ramuz Drive	
7	3d	3d	2d	1½d	1d	1d	Southbourne Grove
8	3½d	3½d	2½d	1½d	1½d	1d	1d	Eastwood Boulevard

Fare Chart 1935.

19. AEC-EEC 120 has been rebuilt to the same design as that depicted in the previous picture. As it waits on stand, the reflection of the overhead junction, where the two sets of overhead wiring seen in Picture 18 meet, is depicted in the upper offside window in this 1950 view. (A T Smith/A B Cross collection)

→ 20. Sister vehicle 119 begins an anti-clockwise circuit on what appears to be a very warm day judging by the open windows. The Victoria Hotel is in the far distance, and the picture is completed with an ex-Wolverhampton trolleybus to the rear, and a Westcliff-on-Sea motorbus on the left. (P Mitchell)

→ 21. In August 1939, Garrett 108 pauses outside the LNER Station, located a short distance further north on the east side of Victoria Avenue; the photographer was in luck as 108 was withdrawn later in 1939. Trolley wheels are fitted for current collection as opposed to the later carbon insert skates, and they are about to pass under a section insulator. The latter were inserted in the overhead every half mile to ensure a failure in one section could be isolated from those adjacent. It was normally the place where electric power was fed into the overhead from substations, as illustrated in this view. (D Thompson)

22. At the same location, an immaculate AEC 124 waits alongside the station forecourt, with an Eastern National motorbus on the right. This view was taken after railway nationalisation, which has left a mixture of railway signage. The notice board and station canopy sign still show LNER, while the one above the motorbus indicates the recently created British Railways. The station was named Victoria to distinguish from the former LMS station, now Southend Central. The notice is advertising an excursion to Rayleigh. (C Carter/LTPS)

➜ 23. This view outside the station looks north along the straight Victoria Avenue, ideal for both tram and trolleybus operation. Sunbeam W 137 (later to become Doncaster 391) has just completed a clockwise circuit of the West Circular, the crew having changed the destination indicator from 28A to 63B at Chalkwell Schools to show that it would continue onto the East Circular. From late in 1951, the two circulars were inter-worked, with initially every other vehicle (later every third) on the West Circular completing a figure-of-eight journey by travelling around the East Circular. The alternating routing was because the west required a higher frequency. Note the Westcliff-on-Sea Motor Services Bristol GO5G motorbus (JN 6895), and the ladies fashion styles. (J Joyce/OTA/Photobus)

➜ 24. This lunchtime view depicts AEC 125 crossing the Blue Boar junction on its way back to town along Victoria Avenue, with the Prittlewell parish church of St Mary the Virgin on the right This was the original reversing terminus for the opening trolleybus service, with the Blue Boar public house behind the photographer. In the background, on the left, is Liddiard's cycle shop advertising the sale of Raleigh and Hercules bicycles; the premises now sell children's wear. (D Gill)

25.   This is the same road junction with the overhead wiring stretching towards Priory Park, and with West Street to the left. In tramway days, cars turned left into West Street, and then along North Road to join London Road. The service was cut back at an early date to near the junction of the former two roads. Trolleybuses on the anti-clockwise West Circular turned left into Fairfax Drive at the bottom of the dip in the distance. The building on the left is "Ye Old Prittlewell Bakery", which dates back to the 16th/17th century, and having undergone restoration, now accommodates an estate agency. The cars approaching are a Ford V8 on the left, and an Austin A70.
(Commercial Postcard/Author's collection)

→   26. Sunbeam 145 (ex-Wolverhampton 265) turns out of Victoria Avenue into Fairfax Drive on the anti-clockwise Service 28B of the West Circular. To the rear, the overhead wiring leading left towards Priory Park can just be seen. This view was taken after trolleybuses had finished on the East Circular in February 1954, as Southend motorbus Daimler 275 is destined for this part of the town. It was purchased as a chassis/part body ex-London Transport (D228) in 1954, fitted with a lowbridge body by Massey Brothers, and entered service with Southend in July 1954. The junction is now controlled by traffic lights and the houses on the right still exist. The bicycle is parked in a very vulnerable position. (D Gill)

→   27. One of the two three axle EEC trolleybuses purchased in 1930, namely 110, is seen in this official view at the Priory Park terminus, the extension from the original Blue Boar turning point of the Prittlewell service; the wiring for the circle can just be seen top right. The destination blind shows Kursaal via the railway stations, which means the vehicle will have travelled along Victoria Avenue, having made its way from the seafront via Marine Parade, Seaway and High Street. Both vehicles were withdrawn in 1939 and passed to Nottingham City Transport for wartime service, becoming 302 and 303 in that fleet. (Omnibus Society collection)

28.   A rear view of the half cabbed AEC-EEC 116, complete with flags and bunting. These were to celebrate the opening of Southend's first illuminations in July 1935. Other trolleybuses and street furniture were also decorated, as some of the subsequent pictures will illustrate. Note the Kursaal advertisement, white licence plate and ornate boom retainer. The location has not been positively identified, but may well be Priory Park. For other views of this interesting vehicle see pictures 57, 99 and 100. (R T Wilson/S Letts/TLRS ©)

WARRIOR SQUARE—CHALKWELL SCHOOLS, VIA FAIRFAX DRIVE.

Leave Warrior Square for Chalkwell Schools, via Fairfax Drive : **Weekdays—**5.23 a.m. and every 10 minutes until 6.53 a.m.   6 58 a.m. and every 5 minutes until 6.38 p.m. 6.48 p.m. and every 10 minutes until 10.08 p.m. **Sundays—**12.53 a.m. and every 10 minutes until 2.03 a.m, 2.08 p.m. and every 5 minutes until 10.08 p.m.

Leave Chalkwell Schools for Warrior Square, via Fairfax Drive : **Weekdays—**5.38 a.m. and every 10 minutes until 7.08 p.m.   7.13 a.m. and every 5 minutes until 6.53 p.m. 7.03 p.m. and every 10 minutes until 10.13 p.m. **Sundays—**1.08 p.m. and every 10 minutes until 2.08 p.m. 2.13 p.m. and every 5 minutes until 10.18 p'm.

WARRIOR SQUARE—CHALKWELL VIA LONDON ROAD.

Leave Warrior Square for Chalkwell Schools, via London Road : **Weekdays—**7.02 a.m. and every 10 minutes until 1.52 p.m. 1.57 p.m. and every 5 minutes until 6.42 p.m. 6.52 p.m. and every 10 minutes until 10.02 p.m. **Sundays—**2.02 p.m. and every 5 minutes until 10.07 p.m.

Leave Chalkwell Schools for Warrior Square via London Road : **Weekdays—**7.12 a.m. and every 10 minutes until 2.02 p.m. 2.07 p.m. and every 5 minutes until 6.52 p.m. 7.02 p.m. and every 10 minutes until 10.22 p.m. **Sundays—**2.07 p.m. and every 5 minutes until 10.22 p.m.

Timetable July 1945. West Circulars operating from Warrior Square.

Fairfax Drive/Cavendish Gardens/Eastwood Boulevard

29.   Garretts 108 and 109 are seen here post 1929 at the end of Fairfax Drive, with Victoria Avenue in the background. Both are in green and cream livery, with 109 carrying a prominent advertisement for the Kursaal. The wiring to the Priory Park terminus can be seen in the background. (Omnibus Society collection)

30.   At the same location, but looking in the opposite direction, Sunbeam 145 (ex-Wolverhampton 265) is seen again with the all-encompassing Victoria Circus destination blind. The shadow of the overhead turnout junction leading to Priory Park can be seen on the road in the foreground. The area to the rear is now the site of the Southend Private Hospital. (D Thompson)

31.   On the opposite side of the road, Sunbeam 144 (ex-Wolverhampton 264) waits at the bus shelter before travelling along Fairfax Drive to Cavendish Gardens. The fenced area to the right was the depot and workshop of Westcliff-on-Sea Motor Services, opened in 1926 to supplement a facility in London Road. After Westcliff was absorbed into Eastern National, it became the latter's Prittlewell depot, but closed in 1981. Following demolition, a new depot was built, which opened in 1987, thus allowing the London Road facility to be closed; this new establishment was vacated in 1991. Note the style of overhead suspension wiring, in this view taken in 1953, with a central vertical dropper in an endeavour to keep the collection wires horizontal. The Southend United Roots Hall football ground is to the rear of the depot. (C Carter/LTPS)

32.   AEC 127 is held at the traffic lights at the end of Fairfax Drive in this 1953 view; it will enter Cavendish Gardens after crossing Southbourne Grove on its anti-clockwise circuit of the West Circular. The windscreen poster indicates the vehicle will pass Chalkwell Park, the venue for some of the Essex County Cricket Club matches. Overhead wiring is carried by both steel and concrete traction standards, and spacing between positive and negative wiring is by offset insulated wire separation; this appeared to be the standard for the Southend system until the use of rigid twin line hangers. The corner shop advertises the Southend Times, published every Wednesday.
(C Carter/LTPS)

33.   AEC 127 is seen again having travelled the length of Fairfax Drive, and now enters the wider section of Cavendish Gardens near Eastwood Boulevard. An Austin car is parked on the left, but there is very little other traffic. Note the connection between the two outer negative wires.
(D Gill)

34.   A little further on AEC 127 now rounds the corner into Nelson Road, with the destination display showing Victoria Circus rather than the West Circular. Before the service was extended along Nelson Road in July 1935, trolleybuses would have turned right at this road junction into Eastwood Boulevard, and almost immediately turned round at its junction with Manchester Drive. (D Thompson)

35.   The crew of AEC-EEC 114 chat as they wait at the Eastwood Boulevard terminus before returning to the Kursaal via the town centre and Seaway, with Westcliff High School in the background. Note the destination indicator in the window at the head of the stairs, and the decorations referred to in Picture 28. Trumans Beer advertisements appeared regularly on Southend's vehicles before the war. (R T Wilson/S Letts/TLRS ©)

Nelson Road/Wellington Avenue

36.   In this view, the domestic property seen on the left in Picture 34 can be seen behind Sunbeam 151 (ex-Wolverhampton 273) as it picks up passengers from the request stop at the beginning of Nelson Road in 1953. The buildings to the left and right comprised the Albany Laundry, with the former now demolished leaving an empty site at the time of writing. The original terminus in Eastwood Boulevard was on the other side of the single storey laundry building.
(C Carter/LTPS)

37.   AEC 128 rounds the bend at the beginning of Nelson Road with the laundry buildings in the background. Comprehensive use of reinforced concrete is illustrated by the road surface and traction standards. (D Gill)

38.   Sunbeam 145 (ex-Wolverhampton 265) travels along Nelson Road as it approaches Chalkwell Schools on London Road. It is about to pass under the overhead crossover from Wellington Avenue on the right, which formed part of the reversing wiring to allow vehicles to return to town. Before the final tram abandonment in 1942, this was the terminus (previously Eastwood Boulevard), but trolleybus wiring was subsequently extended the short distance to London Road, and then into the town centre at Victoria Circus creating the West Circulars. Note the ornate lamppost. (D Thompson)

39.   Here we have a rear view of Sunbeam 147 (ex-Wolverhampton 267) parked in Nelson Road with booms down, having possibly used the Wellington Avenue reverser, which is to the rear of the photographer. The road is deserted other than a single car, and the laundry referred to earlier is in the far distance. Two small boys try to attract the attention of the photographer; does anyone in the Southend area recognise them? The trees lining the road no longer exist. (D Gill)

Southend Trolleybus Extension
   By the Southend-on-Sea Corporation (Trolley Vehicles) Order, 1942, the Minister of War Transport has authorised a section of route some 135 yards in length linking the existing trolleybus route, which terminates in Nelson Road at its junction with Wellington Avenue, with the Leigh tram route, the conversion of which to trolleybus operation has already been authorised. The trolleybus extension authorised is by the way of Nelson Road and London Road, and joins the old tram route at the corner of Leigh Road and London Road.

Newspaper Cutting 28th February 1942.

Nelson Road/London Road

40.　　The solitary Brush bodied utility Sunbeam W 130 is at the end of Nelson Road and about to turn left into London Road at Chalkwell Schools. It has arrived as a 28B, but the crew have made an early blind change to 63A, denoting a cross town service. The vehicle became 384 in the Doncaster Corporation fleet after sale in 1954, and is depicted in Picture 118 with the new owner. (W J Haynes/NTA collection)

WESTERN CIRCULARS
Service 28a.—VICTORIA CIRCUS AND CHALKWELL SCHOOLS (via London Road)

Leave Victoria Circus for Chalkwell Schools; Weekdays—6.48 a.m. and every 5 minutes until 7.28 p.m.; 7.35 p.m. and every 10 minutes until 10.55 p.m. Sundays—7.58 a.m. and every 10 minutes until 10.5ª p.m.
　　Leave Chalkwell Schools for Victoria Circus via Fairfax Drive: Weekdays—5.38 a.m. and every 10 minutes until 6.48 a.m. from Wellington Avenue only. From Schools, 6.57 a.m. and every 5 minutes until 7.37 p.m.; 7.45 p.m. and every 10 minutes until 11.05 p.m. Sundays—9.0ª a.m. and every 10 minutes until 11.07 p.m.
　　Note: Every alternative vehicle from 6.57 a.m. weekdays and 10.7 a.m. Sundays from Chalkwell Schools will proceed to Southchurch and Hamstel Road.

Service 28b.—VICTORIA CIRCUS AND CHALKWELL SCHOOLS (via Fairfax Drive)

Leave Victoria Circus for Chalkwell Schools: Weekdays—5.25 a.m. and every 10 minutes until 6.35 a.m. to Wellington Avenue only. To Schools, 6.45 a.m.; 6.52 and every 5 minutes until 7.22 p.m.; 7.28 p.m. and every 10 minutes until 10.58 p.m. Sundays—8.57 a.m. and every 10 minutes until 10.57 p.m.
　　Leave Chalkwell Schools for Victoria Circus via London Road: Weekdays—7 a.m. and every 5 minutes until 7.35 p.m.; 7.42 p.m. and every 10 minutes until 11.12 p.m. Sundays—9.12 a.m. and every 10 minutes until 11.12 p.m.
　　Note: Every alternate vehicle from 7.05 a.m. weekdays and from 10.02 a.m. Sundays from Chalkwell Schools will proceed to Hamstel Road via North Avenue.

Timetable September 1953. Service numbers now allocated and route integrated with East Circulars. Note early morning short working to Wellington Avenue.

41.   This 1953 view depicts Sunbeam 146 (ex-Wolverhampton 266) turning out of London Road into Nelson Road at Chalkwell Schools, which can just be seen on the extreme right. It is on a clockwise circuit of the West Circular, but has had the destination blind changed to indicate it will complete an anti-clockwise trip round the East Circular after passing through Victoria Circus, thus completing the figure-of-eight circuit. The county cricket notice is carried in the windscreen, and the overhead wiring is spaced using rigid twin line hangers. To the rear is Chalkwell Park where the cricket was played. (C Carter/LTPS)

42.   AEC 124 rounds the bend outside Chalkwell Schools ready to travel along London Road to Victoria Circus during the latter days of the system, with another trolleybus travelling in the opposite direction about to turn right into Nelson Road. A Ford Anglia is pictured to the left, while the scrap man on the right pushes his barrow to his yard or the local merchant. (D Gill)

43. AEC 128 is seen in 1953, complete with county cricket ground notice, outside 636 London Road near to Fleetwood Avenue, and heading towards Chalkwell Schools. At the time, the Essex Health Clinic offered body massage, but new businesses now exist on both sides of the ornate entrance. (C Carter/LTPS)

44. A fine 1950 frontal view of Sunbeam 148 (ex-Wolverhampton 268) as it waits on the northern side of London Road, between the Westcliff-on-Sea Motor Services garage, and the Municipal College. With no driver in view, this is perhaps a layover point before moving into Victoria Avenue to load. (A T Smith/ A B Cross collection)

45.　Having completed an anti-clockwise circuit around the West Circular, Sunbeam W 134 (later to become Doncaster 388) waits on stand at the town end of London Road before crossing Victoria Circus, and then completing a clockwise trip around the East Circular. The wide doorway on the left was the exit from the Westcliff-on-Sea Motor Services garage. This building, and the adjacent former Eastern National garage, were demolished to make way for the current Sainsbury's store, with vehicles being transferred to a new depot in Fairfax Drive built on the former site of the Westcliff premises. (D A Jones/LTPS)

←   46. On the opposite side of the road, with the Municipal College building on the left, Sunbeam W 134 is seen again, and looking as though it has recently left the paint shop. It waits on stand before commencing a clockwise circuit, with the adjacent stop sign providing comprehensive listing of intermediate points. To the rear is Southend AEC motorbus 214, destined for Leigh-on-Sea, on a service operated jointly with Westcliff-on-Sea Motor Services, prior to the full Co-ordination Agreement. (R Marshall collection)

←   47. At the same location, Sunbeam 152 (ex-Wolverhampton 275) awaits departure, with Victoria Circus in the background and with the Municipal College bedecked with flags and bunting. (C Carter/LTPS)

48.   A final view of London Road looking towards Chalkwell, with Victoria Circus to the right of the photographer's position. Significant in this early 1950s view are the number of parked cars of mixed vintage, and the volume of public transport vehicles, which includes two trolleybuses. The exit from the Westcliff-on-Sea Motor Services garage can be seen slightly behind the facing trolleybus. (D Gill)

KURSAAL

The erection of wiring to Marine Parade and the Kursaal from the town centre via Seaway from the Whitegate Road/Bankside reverser gave access to the sea front and all its delights from August 1929. Another access was created to the Kursaal via Southchurch Avenue, when trolleybuses replaced trams in April 1942.

High Street/Marine Parade/Kursaal

49.   This view looks north along High Street, with trolleybus overhead turning into Whitegate Road on the right. Neither trams nor trolleybuses could travel south along High Street towards the pier and sea front because of the low railway bridge immediately behind the photographer, and adjacent to the LMS Station. While trams could reverse in the road, trolleybuses were provided with a reverser along Whitegate Road at its junction with Bankside. This overcame the rejection by the railway company of a turning circle in the station approach, on the left of this picture, and allowed the town end of the Prittlewell/Priory Park service to be extended from Victoria Circus. Subsequently, after lowering of the road under a further railway bridge, wiring was erected along Bankside and Seaway to allow trolleybuses to gain access to the Kursaal along Marine Parade. (Commercial Postcard/Author's collection)

50.   Garrett 109 passes along the newly lowered roadway under the railway bridge in Bankside, which led into Seaway, and to the seafront and the Kursaal. Whitegate Road is in the background, where there was a reverser to allow vehicles to return to the High Street. With the destination blind showing "Special", plus the interest of bystanders, this may well have been the opening trip on this section of the system in August 1929. (S Huxter/Omnibus Society collection)

51.   Garrett 109 leaves the narrow exit, subsequently widened, from Hartington Road (which leads on from Seaway), to enter Marine Parade, presumably on the same inaugural trip seen in Picture 50. Again there is great interest from the general public, with most onlookers wearing headgear. This route extension provided direct access to all the attractions of Marine Parade. (S Huxter/Omnibus Society collection)

52. An immaculate AEC-EEC 120, in lined out livery, waits on the north side of Marine Parade ready to carry out a U turn for the return trip to Priory Park via Seaway and High Street. The combined badges of the EEC winged motif, and the AEC triangle, can be seen on the top of the dummy radiator. The lettering adjacent to the cab door indicates Ben England was the General Manager (1933-36) when the photograph was taken. The gable end of the Ship Hotel can be seen on the extreme left. (J F Higham collection)

➜ 53. At the same location in 1950, Leyland 141 (ex-Tees-side 11) has just passed under a section insulator, and will turn at the Kursaal traffic island ready for the return trip to the town centre. (C Carter/LTPS)

VICTORIA CIRCUS—KURSAAL.

Leave Victoria Circus for Kursaal, via Southchurch Avenue : **Weekdays—** 5.54 a.m. and every 30 minutes until 8.24 a.m. 11.54 a.m. and every 30 minutes until 1.24 p.m. 4.24 p.m. and every 30 minutes until 6.24 p.m.

Leave Kursaal for Victoria Circus, via Southchurch Avenue : **Weekdays—** 6.02 a.m. and every 30 minutes until 8.32 a.m. 12.04 p.m., 12.34 p.m., 1.02 p.m. and 1.32 p.m. 4.32 p.m. and every 30 minutes until 6.02 p.m., then 6.34 p.m.

Leave Victoria Circus for Kursaal, via Seaway : **Weekdays—** 5.39 a.m. and every 30 minutes until 8.39 a.m. 12.09 a.m. and every 30 minutes until 1.39 p.m. 4.09 p.m. and every 30 minutes until 6.39 p.m.

Leave Kursaal for Victoria Circus, via Seaway : **Weekdays—** 5.47 a.m. and every 30 minutes until 8.47 a.m. 12.17 p.m. and every 30 minutes until 1.47 p.m 4.17 p.m. and every 30 minutes until 6.47 p.m.
Sundays—No service.

Timetable July 1945. Two services.

➜ 54. Garrett 105, in original livery, waits to turn round at the Kursaal for the return journey towards the town centre. This view rather emphasises the dated appearance resulting from the protruding driver's cab. Note the horizontal opening windows, and that the usual seaside wares of rock and shellfish are well advertised in the background shops. (J Fielder/Omnibus Society ©)

55.   The original open staircase Garrett 104, now with green between decks (see previous picture) and complete with white wall tyres, waits on the south side of Marine Parade for the return trip to Priory Park. It was the first double deck trolleybus produced by Garrett, and was originally hired by Southend in 1928 to supplement the three single decker trolleybuses running in parallel with trams to Prittlewell. The vehicle was subsequently purchased, and a further five ordered with enclosed staircases. The Kursaal building is on the left, and the Minerva public house on the right is now Tiffins restaurant. The Kursaal was once a vast amusement complex, having been opened in 1901 by the Margate and Southend Kursaal Company, with claims it was the world's first theme park. The word Kursaal is German and means "cure hall" or "spa". It was closed during the second world war, but reopened at the end of hostilities. There was decline in the 1970s, leading to the closure of the amusement area, followed by the building in 1986. After refurbishment the building was reopened in 1998. (A D Packer)

56.   AEC-EEC 114 is seen at the same location, also with white wall tyres; the dummy radiator and piano front gave these vehicles an ungainly appearance. In the right background, there is an advertisement for the Daily Herald, which was the official newspaper of the Labour Party. (W J Haynes/ Omnibus Society collection)

57.   A rare view of the half cabbed ex-EEC/AEC demonstrator 116, taken in July 1935, as it leaves the Kursaal for Priory Park. The three axle chassis was based on the AEC Renown motorbus, with the body and electrical equipment provided by EEC. It was fitted with two staircases, open rear platform and folding front exit; it is seen here in its half cab format, but was rebuilt with full front, and minus the front staircase. After eventual withdrawal, it was converted into a mobile ladies toilet. Note the slip board indicating "To and From Kursaal", and the flags and bunting bedecking the vehicle as described earlier. The shop on the left, behind the attractively decorated traction standard, is selling rock plus hot and cold milk. More details of this vehicle appear in the Rolling Stock section of the book. (R T Wilson/S Letts/TLRS ©)

58. This slightly out of focus pre-war view has been included because of its rarity. It depicts front entrance AEC Q 123, in original lined out green and cream livery, at the Kursaal with the named building on the left. The conductor, complete with summer white cap cover, supervises the queue waiting to board, where it would seem the weather required the wearing of top coats. Note the nearside between decks destination indicator, front lifeguard and light painted traction standards. The vehicle will travel a short distance along Marine Parade and then reach the High Street via Seaway, Bankside and Whitegate Road. (Omnibus Society collection)

59. The driver of bedecked EEC 110, subsequently Nottingham 302, talks to the schoolboy through the open windscreen before returning to Priory Park. The Kursaal tower stands proud to the rear, while on the left is an early local delivery van operated by George and Son Ltd, manufacturing confectioners. Note the front exit and the Estler system of boom mounting, which used a common pivot rather than the side-by-side configuration. (R T Wilson/S Letts/TLRS ©)

60. A rear view of Garrett 109 waiting to make the return trip to town and Priory Park. The vehicle's decorations appear to have been supplemented by the lantern style enhancements around the traction standards. Note the slip board below the rear window and the tower wagon, possibly the Edison battery electric HJ 3148, on the right. (R T Wilson/S Letts/TLRS ©)

61.   At the same location, Leyland 142 (ex-Tees-side 12) waits for the return trip to the town centre in 1950; the open rear platform can just be seen. The sign indicates this is the stop for High Street and Railway Stations; the old Ship Hotel is advertising Truman's Ales, with the landlord at the time being Archie A Wilson. (C Carter/LTPS)

62.   We now move a short distance along Marine Parade, past the turn off to Hartington Road and Seaway leading to the town centre, to the turning circle at the foot of Pier Hill, which was opened in August 1934. Here we see Garrett 106 in July 1935, also decorated with flags and bunting. Use of slip boards is again evident, this time showing "To and From the Pier". Vehicles leaving here were destined for Hamstel Road or Prittlewell, although in post war years this summer spur was not used. Note the advertisements for Southend Super Market (not to be confused with a modern supermarket) and the Tussauds Waxworks, with the current Park Inn Palace hotel on the extreme left. (R T Wilson/S Letts/TLRS ©)

63. This view of the original Garrett 104 clearly shows the open staircase, and was taken on the same day, and in the same place as the previous picture. Flags are mounted above the destination display, with the latter indicating the vehicle is destined for Hamstel Road travelling via Seaway, town centre and North Avenue. Note the licence plate (309) on the left, and the advertisement for Cerebos salt, a brand familiar to current housewives. The road stretches along Marine Parade towards the Kursaal, and on the left the Cambridge Restaurant offers chops and steaks, while the building beyond is the Borough Hotel. (R T Wilson/S Letts/TLRS ©)

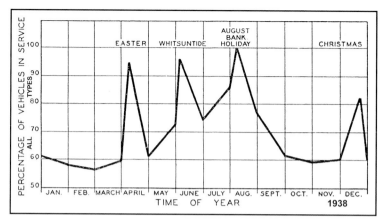

This chart illustrates the difficult seasonal operating conditions of the Southend system.

64.   AEC-EEC 115 waits at the Pier terminus before travelling to Hamstel Road. Originally there were also journeys to Prittlewell from here, but these were discontinued. Some idea of Southend's popularity can be judged from the large number of pedestrians. (Omnibus Society ©)

Southchurch Avenue

65.   This April 1954 view features Sunbeam 149 (ex-Wolverhampton 269) as it rounds the traffic island, which includes a police box, at the Kursaal. Trolleybuses were soon to cease to this destination. Having terminated here on Service 51, it will follow the original tram route along Southchurch Avenue and Southchurch Road back to the town centre. The overhead wiring to the right leads along Marine Parade, and up Seaway to Bankside and the town centre; this was the route of Service 52. (J H Meredith)

66.   Leyland 139 (ex-Tees-side 9) waits at the bottom of Southchurch Avenue before making a return trip to the town centre, having turned round the traffic island seen in the previous picture, which is on the extreme left.   The choice of the name "Radium" for the fish bar must have had some potential customers hesitating before making a purchase.   To the rear is a Bedford HC van. (Omnibus Society ©)

67.   At the same location, AEC-EEC 118, still carrying the dual manufacturers' badging, waits to travel along the length of Southchurch Avenue to its junction with Southchurch Road, and then to the town centre. (D A Jones/ LTPS)

Service 51.—VICTORIA CIRCUS AND KURSAAL
(via Southchurch Avenue)
Leave Victoria Circus for Kursaal : **Mondays to Fridays—7.11** a.m. and every 20 minutes until 10.51 p.m. **Saturdays—7.11 a.m. and** every 20 minutes until 10.51 p.m. **Sundays—9.51 a.m. and every** 20 minutes until 10.51 p.m.
Leave Kursaal for Victoria Circus ; **Mondays to Fridays—** 7.18 a.m. and every 20 minutes until 7.18 p.m.; 7.42 p.m. and every 20 minutes until 11.02 p.m. **Saturdays—7.18 a.m. and every 20** minutes until 10.18 a.m.; 10.42 a.m. and every 20 minutes until 7.22 p.m.; 7.38 p.m. and every 20 minutes until 10.58 p.m. **Sundays—** 9.58 a.m. and every 20 minutes until 10.58 p.m.

Service 52.—SOUTHEND HIGH STREET AND KURSAAL
(via Seaway)
(This Service is Discontinued Until Further Notice)

Timetable September 1953. Route numbers now allocated
and one service discontinued.

68.   Part way down Southchurch Avenue from Southchurch Road, stood the church of St Erkenwald's, which provides the backdrop for this view of Leyland 140 (ex-Tees-side 10) as it makes its way to the Kursaal. The white band on the traction standard is probably a left-over of the wartime enhancement to assist drivers in the blackout. (S Letts)

69.   Seen at the same location, Sunbeam 144 (ex-Wolverhampton 264) is destined for the Kursaal on Service 51. St Erkenwald's church, originally built in 1905, was demolished in 1995, in spite of Grade 2 listed status, and much protestation from the local community.
(A M Wright/NTA collection)

EAST CIRCULAR

The East Circular developed in the following stages:

Stage 1 *From the town centre to Hamstel Road via Bradley Street, Milton Street, Guildford Road, Sutton Road and North Avenue from 31st July 1932.*

Stage 2 *From town centre to Southchurch via Southchurch Road from 3rd April 1944. From North Avenue to Southchurch via Hamstel Road from the same date.*

The picture sequence follows these stages.

Bradley Street to North Avenue/Hamstel Road

70.   Sunbeam W 132 (later to become Doncaster 386) leaves Bradley Street and turns into Victoria Avenue before beginning a clockwise circuit of the West Circular, after first negotiating Victoria Circus to reach London Road. Victoria Station is to the left as the crowds pass the shop advertising the then popular Picture Post magazine. (W J Haynes/NTA collection)

71.   Rebuilt AEC-EEC 114 leaves the East Circular stop just north of Victoria Circus in Victoria Avenue (still showing the former destination) on a short working to Lonsdale Road (via North Avenue), as indicated by the slip board in the nearside windscreen. This short working was created after the East Circular was finally achieved by the wiring of Hamstel Road to Southchurch, after which the original Hamstel Road terminus at the junction with Crossfield Road was dismantled. 114 has just passed under the overhead contact controlling the automatic junction turnout for Bradley Street/Victoria Avenue. (P Mitchell)

HAMSTEL ROAD ROUTE.

Leave Hamstel Road for Victoria Circus, via North Avenue : Weekdays—5.25 a.m., 5.50 a.m., 6.17 a.m. and every 20 minutes until 10.17 p.m. Sundays—As weekdays from 1.17 p.m.

Leave Warrior Square for Hamstel Road, via North Avenue : Weekdays—5.30 a.m. and every 20 minutes until 10.10 p.m. Sundays—As weekdays from 1.10 p.m.

Leave Hamstel Road for Warrior Square, via Southchurch : Weekdays—5.42 a.m. and every 20 minutes until 10.22 p.m. Sundays—As weekdays from 1.02 p.m.

Leave Victoria Circus for Hamstel Road, via Southchurch : Weekdays—5.15 a.m., 5.37 a.m., 6.00 a.m., 6.27 a.m. and every 20 minutes until 10.07 p.m. Sundays—As weekdays from 1.07 p.m.

HAMSTEL ROAD ROUTE.

Leave Warrior Square for Lonsdale Road : Weekdays—10.40 a.m. and every 20 minutes until 6.00 p.m. Sundays—2.40 p.m. and every 20 minutes until 10.00 p.m.

Leave Lonsdale Road for Warrior Square : Weekdays—10.50 a.m. and every 20 minutes until 6.10 p.m. Sundays—2.50 p.m. [and every 20 minutes until 10.10 p.m.

Timetable July 1945. East Circulars plus short working to Lonsdale Road.

72.   AEC 127 waits to turn out of Bradley Street into Victoria Avenue in August 1953, having completed an anti-clockwise circuit. The crew will have changed the destination from a 63B to that displayed at the first stop in North Avenue after Hamstel Road. It has just passed under a section insulator, and a Westcliff-on-Sea Motor Services bus can just be seen in the Victoria Station forecourt. (R F Mack/NTA collection)

73.   Another view of the rare AEC Q 123 in Bradley Street, alongside one of the coal merchant's offices, and on the Hamstel Road service in July 1935. It is suitably bedecked as indicated earlier; note the final destination is missing from the "To and From" slip board position. While the front entrance forward of the leading axle heralds things to come many years later, the lack of a door must have created draughty conditions for the downstairs passengers, particularly in winter. (R T Wilson/S Letts/ TLRS ©)

74.   The driver of Sunbeam W 133 (later Doncaster 387) takes up a position ready to turn left out of a virtually deserted Guildford Road into Sutton Road in 1953, and then onwards to North Avenue on a clockwise circuit. The county cricket ground windscreen display confirms that, having completed the East Circular, 133 will then travel around the West Circular. The shops and cafe on the right have been converted to become "The Guildford" public house, and the three storey building on the left was originally the London Cooperative Society bakery opened in 1921. It still houses a Co-op food store. (C Carter/LTPS)

75.   The bracket armed overhead wiring, stretching from Sutton Road along the length of North Avenue, forms the backdrop for un-rebuilt AEC-EEC 120, which is about to turn left into the former thoroughfare on an anti-clockwise circuit in August 1949. (A D Packer)

76.   The conductor chats to the driver of rebuilt AEC-EEC 121 having completed the reversing manoeuvre at the terminus of the North Avenue short working in Lonsdale Road. The stub end of the reversing overhead is in Durham Road on the right. The destination blind indicates Service 63 to Southchurch, which may be the next trip via North Avenue and the town centre, or the destination blind may be incorrectly set. The windscreen slip board is blank, having been turned over.
(D S Giles/Omnibus Society ©)

Southchurch Road to Southchurch/Hamstel Road

77.   Sunbeam W 138 (later to become Doncaster 392), one of nine utility trolleybuses delivered at the end of the war, is about to depart from the town end of Southchurch Road towards Victoria Circus, as the lady steps carefully on to the pavement. 138 will now travel an anti-clockwise circuit of the West Circular thus completing the figure-of-eight movement. A London Co-operative Society Estate Office is at 129 Southchurch Road on the left next to a florist shop. The buildings on the extreme right no longer exist. (R F Mack)

TROLLEYBUS FARE TABLE.
Hamstel Road Route.

STAGE						
1						Kursaal
2	1d					Whitegate Rd. (Bankside)
3	1d	1d				Southend (L.N.E.R. Stn.)
4	2d	1d	1d			Wimborne Rd.
5	2d	1d	1d	1d		Bournemouth Park Rd.
6	3d	2d	2d	1d	1d	Westbury Rd.
7	3d	2d	2d	2d	1d	1d Hamstel Rd.

Travel to the Southend Stadium by Motorbus or Trolleybus from Victoria Circus.
"Direct to the Entrance Gates."

Tour the Boulevards by Tram this Summer — they are the most beautiful in England.

Fare Chart 1935.

78.	AEC 126, in a rather down at heel condition, is seen in Southchurch Road near the junction with Southchurch Avenue on a return trip to town in spite of the destination display. It was obviously a hot day, with the driver in shirt sleeves, and the half-drop windows lowered. The lower side destination indicator appears to be minus a blind, and the front layout has yet to be modified for the introduction of service numbers circa 1949. The young cyclist looks as though he is about to take advantage of the lack of wind resistance behind the vehicle when it moves off. (C Carter/LTPS)

→	79.	At the same location, and in the same year, passengers leave AEC-EEC 121; the ungainly appearance of these vehicles was greatly improved on those that had the front end rebuilt. The winged EEC radiator motif can be clearly seen, with the AEC badge below, which was a symbol of the two companies' earlier working arrangements. The author first saw these emblems on newly delivered Hastings Tramways AECs during a wartime visit to the seaside town. The destination shows Southend High Street, with the aperture modified ready for the introduction of service number blinds. (C Carter/LTPS)

→	80. The White Horse public house features on the right of this 1953 view as AEC-EEC 114, with rebuilt front end, waits to return to Warrior Square on Service 63. The overhead wiring off to the left leads into Hamstel Road, and then to North Avenue for the circular service. The conductor manually controlled this overhead junction for the left turn; the driver automatically controlled most of the others on the system. The wiring beyond leads to the turning circle, which 114 has just traversed. (C Carter/LTPS)

SOUTHCHURCH—L.M.S. RLY. STA.—WHITEGATE ROAD (Bankside)

Leave Southchurch (White Horse) for L.M.S. Rly. Sta. and Whitegate - Weekdays—7.29 a.m. and every 10 minutes until 6.19 p.m. 6 29 and 6.39 p.m. to Victoria Circus only.   Sundays—2 29 p.m. and every 10 minutes until 10.09 p.m., 10 19 p.m. to Victoria Circus only.

Leave Whitegate Road (Bankside) for Southchurch (White Horse) : Weekdays—7.38 a.m. and every 10 minutes until 6.28 p.m. Sundays—2.38 p m. and every 10 minutes until 1.08 p.m.

Timetable July 1945.

81.   At the same location the unique Gloster 122 waits to return to the town centre on what appears to be a very warm day, given the open windscreen and drop windows. Note the seated passenger to the left of the driver. Early photographs of this vehicle depicted entrance doors (see Picture 101), which appear to have been removed in this view. Due to the position of the entrance the word "Southend" does not appear, just "Corporation Transport", with the coat of arms to the left of the doorway. (D S Giles/Omnibus Society ©)

Timetable September 1953.

Timetable September 1953. Service numbers now allocated and route integrated with West Circulars.

Newspaper Cutting 27th November 1943.

82.   AEC-EEC 121, also with front end rebuilt, turns round at Southchurch in 1953 ready for the return trip to Warrior Square. The turning manoeuvre was across the central reservation of Southchurch Boulevard, the track bed of the earlier popular pre-war circular open toastrack tram service to Thorpe Hall Avenue/Thorpe Bay, and on to the Kursaal. Rigid spaced twin line hangers have been used here; they could also be seen in other areas of the system. (C Carter/LTPS)

83.   Sunbeam W 132 (later Doncaster 386) turns out of Hamstel Road into Southchurch Road on the circular service. The shop on the left carries advertisements for Turf and Craven A cigarettes, plus the attractions of the "True Confessions" magazine; it continues as a newsagents. (D S Giles/Omnibus Society ©)

Thorpe Bay

Trolleybuses replaced trams between the Kursaal and Thorpe Bay from 4th June 1939, but were quickly withdrawn on the outbreak of war until hostilities finished.

84.   The grand houses of Thorpe Bay provide the backdrop for Leyland 139 (ex-Tees-side 9), which looks as though it has recently left the paint shop. (W J Haynes)

85.   The Thorpe Bay turning circle can just be seen in the background, at the junction with Thorpe Hall Avenue, with two trolleybuses waiting to return along the sea front towards the Kursaal. It had been the intention to extend wiring in the Shoeburyness direction, but this never came to pass. In the foreground is Sunbeam 152 (ex- Wolverhampton 275) on an enthusiast special on 17th September 1950, while behind rebuilt AEC-EEC 113 waits on Service 52A. After reaching the Kursaal, it will travel via Marine Parade, Seaway and High Street to Victoria Circus. (J H Meredith)

Southend Coat of Arms granted by Letters Patent in January 1915.

86. This view, probably taken pre-war, depicts AEC-EEC 117 at the Thorpe Bay terminus waiting to travel to Chalkwell Schools via High Street. The two lights each side of the top of the windscreen have been added from the original specification, and the booms are still fitted with trolley wheels rather than the later carbon insert skates. The destination board mounted on the traction standard refers to motorbus services 5A/5B, which ran along the sea front and up Pier Hill to High Street. (Omnibus Society ©)

87. Sunbeam W 130 (later Doncaster 384), the sole Brush bodied utility, waits on the western side of the square before departing to Southchurch via High Street, Victoria Circus and Southchurch Road. The destination aperture has been rebuilt ready for large numbered destination blinds, but temporarily reduced pending their introduction. Trolleybuses rounded this loop in a clockwise direction, while the earlier trams travelled the opposite way. Access to the square was via Southchurch Road (both directions), and also Milton Street from the north. The latter was removed in later years, with doubts if it was ever regularly used on service journeys. This green oasis still remains in spite of all the town centre changes; for a short period in 1942 the car park here was used to disperse some trolleybuses overnight to avoid any potential bomb damage. (P Mitchell)

88. Another view of the square with Sunbeam W 131 (later to become Doncaster 385) waiting to depart on the clockwise East Circular service. Vehicles completing this service entered Warrior Square from Southchurch Road to start another circuit via High Street and Victoria Circus, until the introduction of the figure-of-eight inter working of the two circulars, when vehicles starting the anti-clockwise West Circular continued along Victoria Avenue. Vehicles about to complete a clockwise circuit of the East Circular from the London Road direction passed through Victoria Circus, and then into Bradley Street. Vehicles on the anti-clockwise East Circular turned out of Victoria Circus into Southchurch Road, apart from a period in the early 1950s when they completed a loop around Warrior Square and High Street, before continuing along Southchurch Road. The Milton Street connection allowed inward bound vehicles on the anti-clockwise East Circular to reach the square if required. The square was the town centre terminus for the West circulars for two years from 1944, after which vehicles just passed through Victoria Circus. (P Mitchell)

WARRIOR SQUARE

DEPOT

89.   AEC 127 and Sunbeam 148 (ex-Wolverhampton 268) are seen in the roadway leading from the depot to London Road. The depot buildings are on the left, and the overhead wiring is the final configuration before the system closed. (D Gill)

➔   90. Sunbeams 145 and 149 (ex-Wolverhampton 265 and 269) are parked at the front of Roads 1 and 2 of the extended west side depot building. Overhead wiring out of the building is installed from Roads 1 and 3, with a parking branch from the former, which can be seen top left. (P Mitchell)

➔   91.   Garrett 105 is seen here inside the depot, with the white lines on the left providing guidance to drivers as they move over the inspection pit. Also note the tram track, and the suspended walkways to allow for the cleaning of the upper decks. (D S Giles/Omnibus Society ©)

92. This early view of the entrance to the depot depicts AEC-EEC 112, when new in 1932, under parking Road 8, although Road 5 is the only one wired for trolleybuses at this stage. Note the "No Smoking" and "Car Works" signs, tram track splays and the hut belonging to I Atkinson and Son. (D S Giles/Omnibus Society ©)

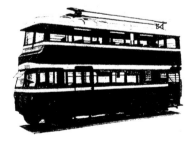

ROLLING STOCK

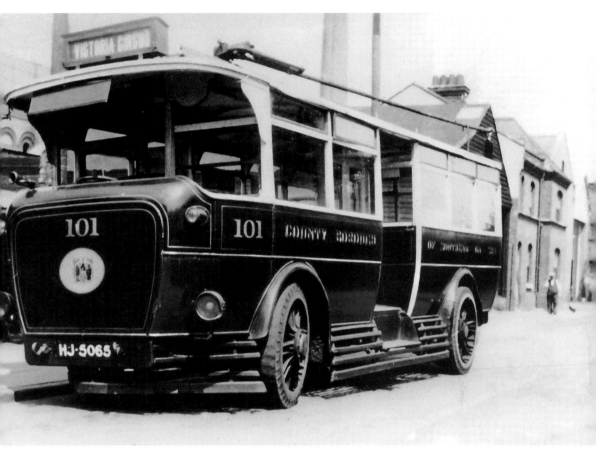

1925   101 (Originally 1)   Railless   HJ 5065
1926   102 (Originally 2)   Railless   HJ 5389

93.   These were the original vehicles used to open Southend's trolleybus system on the Victoria
Circus to Prittlewell service, initially in parallel with the trams. They had EEC electrical equipment,
Short Brothers 29 or 34 seat (possibly increased to 36 seats by 1930) central entrance bodies, and
were fitted with solid tyres and open driving position. They were withdrawn in 1933.
(Omnibus Society collection)

1927   103   AEC 603T (Also designated XU)
NW 9583

1928   104   Garrett OS   HJ 7363 ➜

94.   This vehicle was initially loaned as a demonstrator, having originally operated in Leeds, hence the registration letters. The bodywork, with front entrance and seating 30, is reported as being by Strachan and Brown, and electrical equipment variously reported as BTH or Bull/EMB. It was demonstrated in Oldham and Ashton under Lyne, with reports it was also seen in Bradford, before being initially hired by Southend and purchased in 1928. Withdrawal came in 1937. (Omnibus Society collection)

95.   This vehicle was the first double deck trolleybus purchased, and used to supplement the original low seating single deckers on the Prittlewell service. It was originally hired as a demonstrator and was fitted with a Garrett high-bridge 55 seat body with open staircase; it was exhibited at the 1927 Commercial Motor Show. Electrical equipment comprised a Bull motor and BTH controller. This vehicle proved a success, and an order for five more followed; withdrawal came in 1939. (Omnibus Society collection)

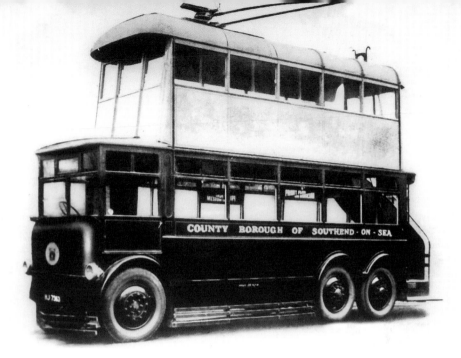

1929 105 - 109 Garrett OS HJ 8925 - 8929 ↓

96.   The follow up delivery came approximately eighteen months later, with the batch being to the same basic design as 104, but with an enclosed staircase and seating 60. These were also withdrawn in 1939. 106 is seen here under tram overhead wiring at the depot, with the positive boom connected, and the negative one held down by the retainer. To operate in this mode, a trailing skate would be required to run in the tram track; if one looks very closely there appears to be such an attachment bottom right. The legal lettering indicates "Southend-on-Sea Corporation Light Railways and Transport Department". (Omnibus Society collection)

1930 110 - 111 English Electric (EEC) JN 60 - 61

97.   The next delivery was two three axle vehicles from EEC, who provided both the electrical equipment and 56 seat highbridge body. 111 is seen here at the manufacturer's works, resplendent in green and cream lined out livery, and with at least one destination blind on display. Note the EEC winged motif and the fitted tow bar; perhaps 111 was being prepared to be towed to Southend. Both were withdrawn in 1939 and passed to Nottingham City Transport the following year, who operated them throughout the war.
(Omnibus Society collection)

1932 112 - 115 AEC 661T/EEC JN 2112 - 2115 →
1933 117 - 121 AEC 661T/EEC JN 2817 - 2821

98.   These nine vehicles saw the trolleybus fleet grow, and were fitted with EEC lowbridge 48 seat bodies, presumably in anticipation the network would extend under low bridges in the area. They had a rather ungainly appearance, with piano front and dummy radiator. Many had the front end rebuilt minus radiator and were given smooth lines, although 112 retained its piano front, but not the dummy radiator. When new (certainly the first batch) they had a skate for use in tram track where there was no negative wiring. It was housed in a locker under the stairs, and could be lowered through a trap door onto the track. This view depicts 112 in pre-war green and cream lined out livery, with the EEC and AEC radiator badges prominent, an indication of the 1930 working agreement between the two companies. They were withdrawn in 1950 and 1954. (Travel Lens Photographic)

1932   116   AEC 663T/EEC   JN 2086

99.   This vehicle was one of three demonstrators created after the 1930 working agreement between AEC and EEC for the manufacture of trolleybuses. Based on an AEC Renown motorbus chassis, it was initially built to a highbridge specification, but had a low overall height due to a front mounted motor and low ceiling height. It carried a Middlesex registration number (HX 1460) as an AEC demonstrator, and was full fronted. In this form, it ran on demonstration in Nottingham during 1930/31 carrying fleet number 26. Because of the difficulty of servicing the front mounted motor, plus structural problems with the body, and changes to the internal height regulations, the vehicle was rebodied. Still carrying the chassis number 663T 001, the highbridge reincarnation comprised a half cab/dummy radiator configuration with an additional front staircase/exit, and seats for 53 or 55. Although referred to as an AEC, the trade press at the time of release referred to the vehicle as being of EEC manufacture, and the photograph above confirms this point. It is believed to have been on trial in Bradford and London, and was exhibited at the 1931 Commercial Motor Show. In the spring of 1932, it came to Southend and was purchased in the November, being re-registered as JN 2086. Also see Pictures 28 and 57. (Author's collection)

↑ 100. Subsequently 116 was rebuilt with full front, front staircase/exit removed as illustrated in this view, and seating increased to 56. After withdrawal in 1950 it was converted into a mobile public toilet (see Picture 120). (W J Haynes/Omnibus Societycollection)

← 1934 122 Gloster TDD JN3822

101.   The Gloucester Carriage and Wagon Company built this unique vehicle, and branded it with the spelling of the city, as indicated in the above heading. It had a highbridge 54 seat central entrance body by the same company, with electrical equipment supplied by Crompton Parkinson and Allen West. It was exhibited at the 1933 Commercial Motor Show, and an article in the February issue of "Passenger Transport" stated it was 15 years ahead of its time, with a low chassis frame and rear mounted motor. It is seen here when new, with the correct destination spelling of its city of origin; withdrawal came in 1950. (Omnibus Society collection)

102.   What a pity this unique trolleybus could not have been preserved; 122 awaits disposal following withdrawal. (Omnibus Society ©)

1934 123 AEC Q 761T JN4373

103.   This was another rare vehicle, being one of only five built to this design, with UK operators purchasing only two. The chassis was a development of the AEC Q motorbus, which had a side mounted engine and set back front axle, allowing a front entrance opposite the driver, much as today's specifications. The lowbridge body and electrical equipment were by EEC, with the former accommodating 56 seats. The other UK purchaser was Bradford, the balance going to Sydney, Australia. After withdrawal in 1949, it became a mobile radar unit at Southend Airport following removal of the top deck. 123 is seen here opposite Chalkwell Park outside a store selling Manns beer; an estate agent now occupies the building. (W J Haynes)

104.   The vehicle is seen here in original lined out pre-war livery in the depot yard. The front entrance, set back front axle and short rear overhang are well illustrated. The destination is of interest as this photograph was taken before the wartime conversion of London Road to trolleybus operation, and probably referred to the Wellington Avenue reverser near Chalkwell Schools. (J Manning/Omnibus Society collection)

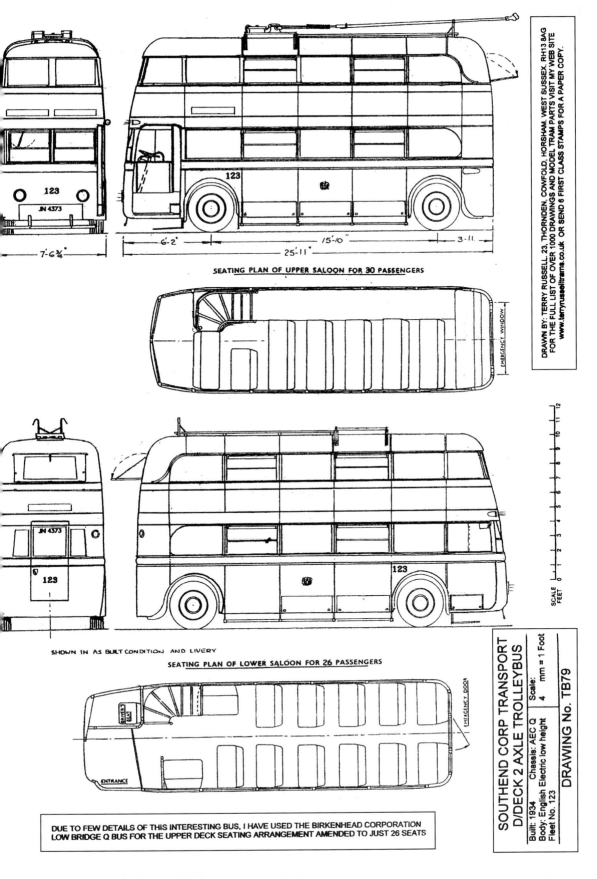

123

JN 4373

7'-6¾"

6'-2"   15'-10"   3'-11"

25'-11"

EMERGENCY WINDOW

SEATING PLAN OF UPPER SALOON FOR 30 PASSENGERS

123

SCALE FEET 0 1 2 3 4 5 6 7 8 9 10 11 12

JN 4373

123

123

SHOWN IN AS BUILT CONDITION AND LIVERY

SEATING PLAN OF LOWER SALOON FOR 26 PASSENGERS

DRIVER'S SEAT

EMERGENCY DOOR

ENTRANCE

DRAWN BY: TERRY RUSSELL, 23, THORNDEN, COWFOLD, HORSHAM, WEST SUSSEX. RH13 8AG
FOR THE FULL LIST OF OVER 1000 DRAWINGS AND MODEL TRAM PARTS VISIT MY WEB SITE
www.terryrusselltrams.co.uk OR SEND 6 FIRST CLASS STAMPS FOR A PAPER COPY.

SOUTHEND CORP TRANSPORT
D/DECK 2 AXLE TROLLEYBUS

Built: 1934	Chassis: AEC Q	Scale:
Body: English Electric low height		4 mm = 1 Foot
Fleet No. 123		

DRAWING No. TB79

DUE TO FEW DETAILS OF THIS INTERESTING BUS, I HAVE USED THE BIRKENHEAD CORPORATION
LOW BRIDGE Q BUS FOR THE UPPER DECK SEATING ARRANGEMENT AMENDED TO JUST 26 SEATS

105. The final demise of 123 as it awaits disposal to Southend Airport in 1950. To the right, withdrawn and minus engine, is one of the four AEC Regent motorbuses ex-Mansfield District Traction, acquired in 1946 as a short term post war stopgap. (Omnibus Society collection)

1939   124 - 129   AEC 661T   BHJ 194 - 199 ➜

106.   Southend was fortunate to receive these six vehicles just before the outbreak of the 1939-1945 war. They were fitted with Strachan 56 seat highbridge bodies, and carried EEC electrical equipment. 124-127 were loaned to Bradford City Transport from September 1940 to February 1942 as indicated later (see Picture 115). Withdrawal came in 1954; it had been hoped to sell five to a Spanish operator, but this fell through and they were scrapped. 126 is seen here at the end of London Road, with Victoria Circus in the background. (R Marshall)

1945	130	Sunbeam W	BHJ 827	Brush Utility Highbridge Body ➜
	131 - 132	Sunbeam W	BHJ 828 - 829	Park Royal Utility H/Bridge Body
1946	133 - 138	Sunbeam W	BHJ 898 - 903	Park Royal Utility H/Bridge Body

107.   These nine utility vehicles, hence the W chassis designation, arrived in the immediate post war period, and were fitted with BTH motors, and 56 seat highbridge bodies to a relaxed Ministry specification. Withdrawal came in 1953, and the whole batch was acquired by Doncaster Corporation, becoming 384-392 in their fleet. They entered service with their new owner in 1954, and received new Roe 62 seat bodies between 1957 and 1959. After eventual withdrawal in 1961/62, these bodies were converted to half cab configuration and mounted on Daimler motorbus chassis. 133 is seen here in immaculate condition; also see Pictures 118 and 119 depicting vehicles while in Doncaster. (D S Giles/Omnibus Society ©)

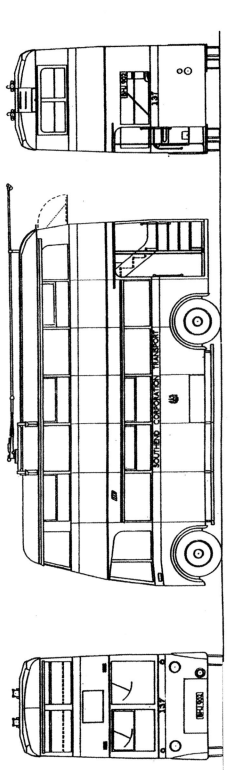

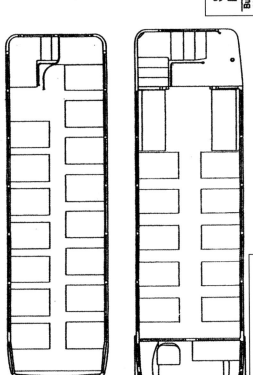

SOUTHEND CORP TRANSPORT
D/DECK 4 WHEEL TROLLEYBUS

Scale:
4 mm = 1 Foot

Built: Park Royal 1945/46
Chassis: Karrier W4
Fleet No. 133 -138

DRAWING No. TB78

SCALE
FEET
0 1 2 3 4 5 6 7 8 9 10 11 12

DRAWN BY: TERRY RUSSELL, 23. THORNDEN, COWFOLD, HORSHAM, WEST SUSSEX. RH13 8AG
FOR THE FULL LIST OF OVER 1000 DRAWINGS AND MODEL TRAM PARTS VISIT MY WEB SITE
www.terryrusselltrams.co.uk OR SEND 8 FIRST CLASS STAMPS FOR A PAPER COPY.

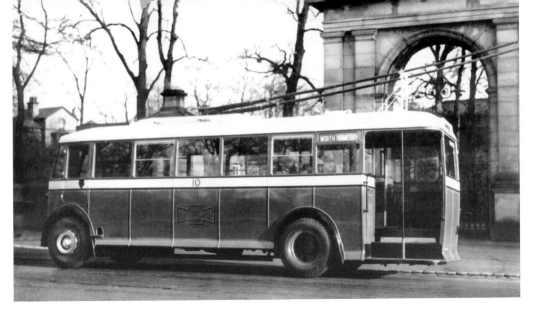

1946   139 - 143   Leyland TB 3   VN 9434 - 9438

108.   With the growth of traffic in the immediate post war period, this batch of single deck vehicles was acquired ex-Tees-side Railless Traction Board, via bus dealer North's of Leeds, and were numbered 9-13 in their fleet. They had open rear entrance 32 seat bodies by Massey Brothers, the latter being a foretaste of Southend's use of this bodybuilder for many of its post war motorbuses. GEC electrical equipment was fitted, and they were withdrawn in 1952 having been new to Tees-side in 1936; one became the feature of a children's playground in Priory Park. 140 (ex-Tees-side 10) is seen here before delivery to its original owner, giving a clear view of the open platform. (Massey/P Battersby collection)

1950   144 - 152   Sunbeam MF2   BDA 364 - 369/BJW 171/173/175

109.   A further batch of second hand vehicles was acquired ex-Wolverhampton Corporation; they were numbered 264-269/271/273/275 in the fleet, and dated from 1938. They had BTH electrical equipment and were fitted with Park Royal 54 seat highbridge bodies. While being cheap to purchase, they proved expensive to overhaul before entering service with Southend, and withdrawal came in 1953/54. 265 and 264 (Southend 145 and 144) await the attention of Southend's workshop staff. (R Sims/Omnibus Society collection)

TOWER WAGONS

110.   This view of tower wagon 5 (HJ 8969) depicts one of two Tilling Stevens units used to service the tram and trolleybus systems. 5 was a TSB 39, while the other numbered 6 (HJ 9165) was a TS4. An earlier Edison battery electric tower wagon (HJ 3148) was probably used in the early days of trolleybus operation. (D S Giles/Omnibus Society ©)

111.   This view of AEC 127, taken in 1950, has been included, as it has hit a spot of bother as it leaves Victoria Circus and enters London Road. The left hand boom is pointing up towards the last upper storey window of the Dixon's store, and Karrier tower wagon 8 (BHJ 528) is in attendance. (A B Cross)

112.   The overhead linesmen attend to the boom of Sunbeam W 130 (later Doncaster 384) working from the tower of Karrier BHJ 528. Note the slip board in the nearside windscreen indicating the destination is Wellington Avenue, the short working terminus of the West Circular near to Chalkwell Schools. (D S Giles/Omnibus Society ©)

GUY DEMONSTATOR

113.   Southend hired a six wheel Guy BTX from Guy Motors in the second half of 1934, and may have given it fleet number 124, which was used for the first of the 1939 AEC delivery. It was a demonstrator, and carried a Wolverhampton registration number (JW 5370), which was the home of the Guy factory. It began operation with South Lancashire Transport in 1935 when it was five years old, although the registration was from 1934, and was given fleet number 47. GEC electrical equipment was fitted, and the highbridge 56 seat body was also by Guy; there are reports that the vehicle had been in South Africa before its UK registration. Here we see 47 on the extreme left, in a line up of South Lancashire vehicles in Atherton depot yard. While with this operator the front was rebuilt to a design similar to the other vehicles in the view, and the livery was red and cream. (R Hannay)

→   114.   A rare view of Durban Leyland TB2 22, in a grey and cream livery, and on trial on the Southend system. This vehicle, together with ten others, plus eleven Sunbeams, was used on the Durban system, which opened on 22nd February 1935. 22 is seen here leaving the Eastwood Boulevard terminus. Evidence to support this conclusion is that the trolleybus at the terminus in the background has the Southend livery, complete with destination indicator in the second rearward upper window, and the Trumans advertisement widely used on Southend's vehicles at the

SOUTH AFRICAN VISITOR

time. A second unused photograph indicates an Eastwood Boulevard road sign, and the Westcliff High School building in the distant background. 22 was fitted with a Park Royal body, and GEC electrical equipment. (S Lockwood collection)

LOAN ASSIGNMENT

115.   Four of the 1939 delivery of AEC trolleybuses were loaned to Bradford City Transport for nearly eighteen months from September 1940 to February 1942. The four were 124-127, and the former is seen in Forster Square, Bradford, with white lower front panel and lifeguard, plus masked headlights, all a wartime requirement. 124 was released from Bradford works for service on 4th September 1940, and returned to be prepared for its move to Southend on 2nd February 1942; the journey home was on the 23rd February. General maintenance was carried out during its stay in Yorkshire, with a motor overhaul in June 1941. The four vehicles were based at the Saltaire depot, and after initial training were used on the City/Saltaire/Crossflatts service. A blue and cream livery was adopted by Bradford, believed to have been inspired by the Southend vehicles, and first appearing on their newly delivered utility Sunbeams 693-702 (ex Johannesburg chassis) of 1942, plus the repainting of existing AEC 671. This is the only known photograph of one of the loaned vehicles in Bradford. (S King)

SYSTEM CLOSURE

116.   AEC 128 waits in the depot roadway, suitably bedecked with flags and bunting, ready for the formal closure of the system on 28th October 1954, although scheduled services had ceased the day before. So ended just over 53 years of electrically powered public street transport in the town, with trolleybuses having operated 29 of them. (D Gill)

More local history can be found in: *Southend-on-Sea Tramways*, which includes the Pier Electric Railway, *Branch Lines to Southend and Southminster* and *Barking to Southend*, which includes Shoeburyness.

THE AFTER LIFE

117.   English Electric 110 and 111 were withdrawn in 1939 and passed to Nottingham City Transport, becoming 302 and 303 in their fleet, where they served the new owners throughout the war until 1946. 302 is parked on Victoria Embankment in green and cream livery, with wartime white painted areas and masked headlights. Nottingham's Trent Bridge depot and works is around the corner on the right in Banbury Street. One destination indicator has been retained, but the other is removed to make way for a route number box. (Omnibus Society collection)

118. The sole Brush bodied Southend utility Sunbeam W 130 is depicted here after being sold to Doncaster, and is operating in its original form. It has received the Doncaster livery, and is numbered 384 in their fleet; it was rebodied in 1959. The vehicle is returning to the town centre from Bentley, whose parish church of St Peter can be seen in the background. The Doncaster destination blinds indicated the outer terminus, even on the return trip to the town centre. (R Marshall)

119.   All the Southend utility Sunbeam W trolleybuses purchased by Doncaster Corporation were rebodied by Roe between 1957 and 1959.   Here Doncaster 388 (Southend 134) is seen in its rejuvenated form waiting at the town centre stand in West Laith Gate before departing to Balby. From about 1955, the Doncaster livery was red with a single white band. (Author's collection)

120.   Having had one rebuild, AEC 116 received a further make-over after withdrawal, with conversion to a mobile ladies toilet for use by the Corporation at various events. Southend also converted a second vehicle to a similar format, this time using a three axle motorbus (originally a trolleybus) ex-Bournemouth Corporation (LJ 7702). The Southend conversion seen below was numbered 1, and the ex-Bournemouth vehicle was 2. Note the water storage tank mounted on the roof, with pipe work feeding the WCs. (R F Mack/NTA collection)

MP Middleton Press
EVOLVING THE ULTIMATE RAIL ENCYCLOPEDIA

Easebourne Lane, Midhurst, West Suss
GU29 9AZ   Tel:01730 813169
email:info@middletonpress.co.uk

ISBN PREFIXES - A-978 0 906520   B- 978 1 873793   C- 978 1 901706   D-978 1 904474   E - 978 1 906008

* BROCHURE AVAILABLE SHOWING RAILWAY ALBUMS AND NEW TITLES *

ORDER ONLINE - *PLEASE VISIT OUR WEBSITE* - www.middletonpress.co.u

TRAMWAY CLASSICS *Editor Robert J Harley*

Aldgate & Stepney Tramways to Hackney and West India Docks	B 70 1
Barnet & Finchley Tramways to Golders Green and Highgate	B 93 0
Bath Tramways Peter Davey and Paul Welland	B 86 2
Blackpool Tramways 1933-66 75 years of Streamliners Stephen Lockwood	E 34 5
Bournemouth & Poole Tramways Roy C Anderson	B 47 3
Brightons Tramways The Corporation's routes plus lines to Shoreham and to Rottingdean	B 02 2
Bristol's Tramways A massive system radiating to ten destinations Peter Davey	B 57 2
Burton & Ashby Tramways An often rural light railway Peter M White	C 51 2
Camberwell & West Norwood Trys including Herne Hill and Peckham Rye	B 22 0
Chester Tramways Barry M Marsden	E 04 8
Chesterfield Tramways a typical provincial system Barry Marsden	D 37 1
Clapham & Streatham Tramways including Tooting and Earlsfield J.Gent & J.Meredith	B 97 8
Croydons Tramways J.Gent & J.Meredith including Crystal Palace, Mitcham and Sutton	B 42 8
Derby Tramways a comprehensive city system Colin Barker	D 17 3
Dover's Tramways to River and Maxton	B 24 4
East Ham & West Ham Trys from Stratford and Ilford down to the docks	B 52 7
Edgware & Willesden Tramways including Sudbury, Paddington & Acton	C 18 5
Embankment & Waterloo Trys including the fondly remembered Kingsway Subway	B 41 1
Enfield and Wood Green Tramways Dave Jones	C 03 1
Exeter & Taunton Tramways Two charming small systems J B Perkin	B 32 9
Fulwell - Home for Trams, Trolleys and Buses Professor Bryan Woodriff	D 11 1
Gosport & Horndean Tramways Martin Petch	B 92 3
Great Yarmouth Tramways A seaside pleasure trip Dave Mackley	D 13 5
Hammersmith & Hounslow Trys branches to Hanwell, Acton & Shepherds Bush	C 33 8
Hampstead & Highgate Trys from Tottenham Court Road and King's Cross Dave Jones	B 53 4
Hastings Tramways A sea front and rural ride	B 18 3
Holborn & Finsbury Trys Angel-Balls Pond Road - Moorgate - Bloomsbury	B 79 4
Huddersfield Tramways the original municipal system Stephen Lockwood	D 95 1
Hull Tramways Level crossings and bridges abound Paul Morfitt & Malcolm Wells	D 60 9
Ilford & Barking Tramways to Barkingside, Chadwell Heath and Beckton	B 61 9
Ilkeston & Glossop Tramways Barry M Marsden	D 40 1
Ipswich Tramways Colin Barker	E 55 0
Keighley Tramways & Trolleybuses Barry M Marsden	D 83 8
Kingston & Wimbledon Trys incl Hampton Court, Tooting & four routes from Kingston	B 56 5
Liverpool Tramways - 1 Eastern Routes	C 04 8
Liverpool Tramways - 2 Southern Routes	C 23 9
Liverpool Tramways - 3 Northern Routes A trilogy by Brian Martin	C 46 8
Llandudno & Colwyn Bay Tramways Stephen Lockwood	E 17 8
Lowestoft Tramways a seaside system David Mackley	E 74 1
Maidstone & Chatham Trys from Barming to Loose and from Strood to Rainham	B 40 4
Margate & Ramsgate Tramways including Broadstairs	C 52 9
North Kent Tramways including Bexley, Erith, Dartford, Gravesend and Sheerness	B 44 2
Norwich Tramways A popular system comprising ten main routes David Mackley	C 40 6
Nottinghamshire & Derbyshire Try including the Matlock Cable Tramway Barry M Marsden	D 53 1
Portsmouth Tramways including Southsea Martin Petch	B 72 5
Plymouth and Torquay Trys including Babbacombe Cliff Lift Roy Anderson	E 97 0

Reading Tramways Three routes - a comprehensive coverage Edgar Jordon	B 8
Scarborough Tramway including the Scarborough Cliff Lifts Barry M Marsden	E 1
Seaton & Eastbourne Tramways Attractive miniature lines	B 7
Shepherds Bush & Uxbridge Tramways including Ealing John C Gillham	C 2
Southampton Tramways Martin Petch	B 3
Southend-on-Sea Tramways including the Pier Electric Railway	B 2
South London Tramways 1903-33 Wandsworth - Dartford	D
South London Tramways 1933-52 The Thames to Croydon	D 8
Southwark & Deptford Tramways including the Old Kent Road	B 3
Stamford Hill Tramways including Stoke Newington and Liverpool Street	B 8
Triumphant Tramways of England Stephen Lockwood FULL COLOUR	E 6
Twickenham & Kingston Trys extending to Richmond Bridge and Wimbledon	C 3
Victoria & Lambeth Tramways to Nine Elms, Brixton and Kennington	B 4
Waltham Cross & Edmonton Trys to Finsbury Park, Wood Green and Enfield	C 0
Walthamstow & Leyton Trys including Clapton, Chingford Hill and Woodford	B 6
Wandsworth & Battersea Trys from Hammersmith, Putney and Chelsea	B 6
York Tramways & Trolleybuses Barry M Marsden	D 8

TROLLEYBUSES *(all limp covers)*

Birmingham Trolleybuses ... David Harvey	E 1
Bournemouth Trolleybuses ... Malcolm N Pearce	C 1
Bradford Trolleybuses ... Stephen Lockwood	D 1
Brighton Trolleybuses ... Andrew Henbest	D 3
Cardiff Trolleybuses ... Stephen Lockwood	D 4
Chesterfield Trolleybuses ... Barry M Marsden	D 5
Croydon Trolleybuses ... Terry Russell	B 7
Darlington Trolleybuses ... Stephen Lockwood	D 3
Derby Trolleybuses ... Colin Barker	C 7
Doncaster Trolleybuses ... Colin Barker	E 9
Grimsby & Cleethorpes Trolleybuses ... Colin Barker	D 8
Hastings Trolleybuses ... Lyndon W Rowe	B 8
Huddersfield Trolleybuses ... Stephen Lockwood	C 9
Hull Trolleybuses ... Paul Morfitt and Malcolm Wells	D 2
Ipswich Trolleybuses ... Colin Barker	D 5
Maidstone Trolleybuses ... Robert J Harley	C 0
Manchester & Ashton Trolleybuses ... Stephen Lockwood	E7
Mexborough & Swinton Trolleybuses ... Colin Barker	E 3
Newcastle Trolleybuses ... Stephen Lockwood	D 7
Nottinghamshire & Derbyshire Trolleybuses ... Barry M Marsden	D
Portsmouth Trolleybuses ... Barry Cox	C 7
Reading Trolleybuses ... David Hall	C 0
South Lancashire Trolleybuses ... Stephen Lockwood	F 3
South Shields Trolleybuses ... Stephen Lockwood	E 1
Southend Trolleybuses ... Colin Barker	F 2
Tees-side Trolleybuses ... Stephen Lockwood	D 5
Wolverhampton Trolleybuses 1961-67 ... Graham Sidwell	D 8
Woolwich and Dartford Trolleybuses ... Robert J Harley	B 6